INTER-COLONIAL RAILWAY.

MAY IT PLEASE YOUR EXCELLENCY,—

The papers laid before the Legislature, during the last Session, brought down the history of the Intercolonial Railway negociation to the period when the Delegates from the three Provinces left England in January 1862. We have now the honor to detail the steps subsequently taken until the close of the negociations at Quebec.

On the 30th April, a Despatch from His Grace the Duke of Newcastle was received by Your Excellency, and which, as it led to the discussions and arrangements that it becomes our duty to explain, we insert at length:

Nova Scotia.—No. 155.

Downing Street,
12th April, 1862.

MY LORD,—

I have already acknowledged the receipt of Your Lordship's Despatches, the one accompanied by a joint address to Her Majesty from both Houses of the Legislature of Nova Scotia, expressive of their wish that Imperial aid may be afforded to the completion of the Inter-Colonial Railway between Halifax and Quebec; the other reporting that the Honorable Joseph Howe had been appointed to represent Nova Scotia in the Provincial Delegation which was intended to visit England on the subject.

Not long afterwards Mr. Howe arrived, and associated himself with the Honorable Mr. Vankoughnet, who had been appointed Delegate on behalf of Canada, and the Honorable Samuel Tilley, on behalf of New Brunswick.

I had several interviews with those gentlemen, who urged with great ability the project committed to their charge, and eventually embodied their views in a memorandum communicated to me in a letter dated the 2nd of December, 1861. But, owing to the urgency of business connected with the threatening aspect of affairs in the United States, I was unable to bring the subject under the consideration of Her Majesty's Government before the Deputies were obliged to return to their homes; and other urgent matters have hitherto prevented the adoption of a decision. The subject has now been before Her Majesty's Government, and I need scarcely assure you that they have examined it with the care due to the importance of the question, to the high authorities from whom it has emanated in the Provinces, and to the character and position of the Delegates by whom it has been so powerfully presented to notice in this country.

The length of Railway necessary to complete the communication between Halifax and Quebec, is estimated at 350 miles, and the cost, after deducting the right of way, which the Provinces will provide, is estimated at Three Millions Sterling. Such being the data supplied by the deputation, the project is, that the Imperial Government shall join the three Provinces in a guarantee of four per cent upon three millions of pounds, in which case the Provinces are ready to pass Bills of Supply for sixty thousand pounds a year (twenty thousand pounds in each Province) if the Imperial Government will do the same. The selection of the route is left solely to the British Government. Should the sum of three millions be found insufficient, nothing very definite is said on the essential point of the provision to be made for the completion of the Railway.

I much regret to inform you, that after giving the subject their best consideration, Her Majesty's Government have not felt themselves at liberty to concur in this mode of assistance.

Anxious, however, to promote as far as they can the important object of completing the great line of Railway communication on British ground, between the Atlantic and the Westernmost parts of Canada, and to assist the Provinces in a scheme which would so materially promote their interests, Her Majesty's Government are willing to offer to the Provincial Governments, an Imperial guarantee of interest, towards enabling them to raise by public loan, if they should desire it, at a moderate rate, the requisite funds for constructing the Railway. This was the mode of action contemplated by Earl Grey in the year 1851, and is the same method which was adopted by Parliament in the act of 1842, in order to afford Canada the benefit of British credit in raising the money with which she has completed her great system of internal water communications.

The nature and extent of the guarantee which Her Majesty's Government would undertake to recommend to Parliament, must be determined by the particulars of any scheme which the Provincial Governments may be disposed to found on the present proposal, and on the kind of security which they would offer.

I fear that this course will not be so acceptable to the Provincial Governments as that which the Delegates were authorized to propose for consideration. It is, however, the only one in which Her Majesty's Government, after anxious deliberation, feel that they would be at liberty to participate. I trust that the proposal will at all events be received as a proof of their earnest wish, to find some method in which they can co-operate with the Provinces, in their laudable desire to complete a perfect Intercolonial communication over British Territory; and it will be a source of sincere pleasure to me, if, adverting to all the different bearings of the subject, and to the condition of their respective finances, the Provincial Governments should end by finding it in their power to make use of the present offer, and to propound some practicable scheme for applying it to the attainment of the desired object.

I have addressed a similar despatch to the Governor-General of Canada and the Lieutenant-Governor of New Brunswick; and I must now leave the subject in the hands of the several Provincial Governments, who will best know, in case they prosecute the subject further, how to provide for the requisite mutual consultations.

I have the honor to be,
My Lord,
Your Lordship's most obedient,
Humble servant,
(Signed) NEWCASTLE.

Lieutenant-Governor
The Right Honorable
THE EARL OF MULGRAVE.

As the proposition submitted by Her Majesty's Government involved, if accepted, a Colonial liability so much larger than that which had been contemplated when the offer of the Provinces was made, the first impression left by its perusal here was, that all negociations must now terminate, unless Canada would consent to assume a much larger proportion of the cost of the work than one-third of the whole. To ascertain if there was any probability of this being done, Mr. Howe and Mr. Tilley went to Quebec in June. They discussed the subject with His Excellency the Governor-General, and with the three members of the Cabinet who were at the Capital, and frankly explained to them, that the acceptance of the proposal was impossible, if the Maritime Provinces were expected to provide for two-thirds of the sum required. This did not seem to be expected, and Lord Monk and his Ministers expressed a desire to have the whole subject reviewed in a Conference to be held at Quebec in September, when it was understood that Your Excellency and the Lieutenant-Governor of New Brunswick were to visit that city. The following Despatch was subsequently received here, fixing the date of the Conference:

(COPY.)

Government House, Quebec,
15th August, 1862.

MY LORD,—

In a Despatch which I have received from the Duke of Newcastle, dated April 12th, 1862, containing the conditions under which Her Majesty's Government propose to assist the Colonies in the construction of a railway connecting Halifax with Riviere du Loup, His Grace mentions that he had sent, at the same time, identical Despatches, to your Excellency and the Lieutenant Governor of New Brunswick.

It is very desirable, in order to return a satisfactory answer to the Despatch in question, that the Ministers of the three Provinces interested—Canada, New Brunswick, and Nova Scotia—should come to a distinct understanding as to the part which each of these Provinces will undertake in reference to the execution of the proposed work. I think this end will be best obtained, by a personal conference between the members of the administrations of the three Provinces.

I am aware that it is the intention of your Excellency to visit Canada in the beginning of next month, and I expect the Lieutenant Governor of New Brunswick will be here about the same time.

It appears to me, therefore, that the time which I have mentioned offers peculiar advantages for holding the proposed consultation; and I shall feel much obliged if your Excellency will arrange with such members of your administration as may be deputed to assist at the conference, to attend at Quebec on Wednesday, September 10th, for that purpose.

The question of intercolonial trade will probably be discussed at the same time.

I have addressed a Despatch of the same import as this communication to the Lieutenant Governor of New Brunswick.

I have, &c.

(Signed) MONK.

His Excellency,
THE EARL OF MULGRAVE, &c. &c. &c.

The undersigned having been selected by Your Excellency to represent the Province of Nova Scotia, repaired to Quebec accordingly, and were invited, with Mr. Annand, who had gone to Canada on a separate mission, touching questions of intercolonial trade, to take seats at the Council Board. The Hon. Messrs. Tilley, Mitchell, and Steves, members of the Executive Council of New Brunswick, were also present. The Conference lasted three days, and was conducted with great freedom, but in a moderate and conciliatory spirit, honourable to the Provinces, and full of promise of satisfactory results.

Having discussed with the gentlemen present, the immediate question which had brought us together, and all collateral questions growing out of it — of commerce, postal subsidies, immigration and political union — the Delegates from the maritime Provinces professed their willingness to propose to their respective Governments to accept the proposition of the Duke of Newcastle, if the Government of Canada would bear one half of the expense, instead of one-third.

Looking to the extent, population, and resources of Canada, as compared with those of the Lower Provinces, this did not seem to be be a disproportionate share. Looking to the facility with which they could be defended by sea and land at all seasons of the year, and to the imperative necessity for the Intercolonial Railway, as a work of defence for Canada in winter, it appeared to the undersigned that the offer was fair, if not generous.

After a day's deliberation, the Canadian Council communicated their ultimatum, which was an offer to assume five-twelfths of the liability of constructing and working the Intercolonial Railroad, provided that the other Provinces would assume the other seven-twelfths.

To accept or to reject this proposition imposed upon the gentlemen to whom it was made a very grave responsibility. To reject it, was to postpone indefinitely, perhaps forever, the construction of a work of acknowledged value, whether the defence or the development of the resources and elevation of all the Provinces were concerned; and to accept it, in the face of existing liabilities and the cost to be incurred, was a step so grave, that it could not be lightly taken. After serious and anxious deliberation, the Delegates from Nova Scotia and New Brunswick decided to assume the responsibility: and it was satisfactory to us to know, that when communicated, your Excellency and the Hon. Mr. Gordon approved of the decision.

Accord, upon the main point, having been established, it became necessary to adjust some questions indispensable to the harmonious action of the three Governments, and to the further progress of the negociation. The results of our deliberations upon these points, are included in the following Memoranda:

(Copy.)

NO. 1 MEMORANDUM.

The undersigned, representing the three Governments of Canada, Nova Scotia, and New Brunswick, convened to consider the Despatch of His Grace the Duke of Newcastle of the 12th April, 1862, with reference to the Intercolonial Railway, having given the very important matters contained in that Despatch their attentive consideration, are agreed:

I. That whilst they have learned with very great regret that Her Majesty's Imperial Government has finally declined to sanction the proposal made on behalf of these Provinces in December, 1861, and at previous periods, they at the same time acknowledge the consideration exhibited in substituting the proposal of "an Imperial guarantee of interest towards "enabling them to raise by public loan, if they should desire it, at a "moderate rate, the requisite funds for constructing the Railway."

II. That, with an anxious desire to bind the Provinces more closely together, to strengthen the connexion with the mother country, to promote their common commercial interest, and to provide facilities essential to public defences of these Provinces as integral parts of the Empire, the undersigned are prepared to assume, under the Imperial guarantee, the liability for the expenditure necessary to construct this great work.

III. That the three Governments are agreed, that the proportion of liability for the necessary expenditure, shall be apportioned as follows, namely: five-twelfths for Canada, and seven-twelfths to be equally divided between the Provinces of New Brunswick and Nova Scotia.

IV. But it is understood, that the liability for principal and interest shall be borne by each Province, to the extent only of the proportion hereby agreed upon.

V. That, in arriving at this conclusion, the undersigned have been greatly influenced by the conviction, that the construction of the Road between Halifax and Quebec must supply an essential link in the chain of an unbroken highway extending through British territory from the Atlantic to the Pacific, in the completion of which, every Imperial interest in North America is most deeply involved: and the undersigned are agreed that to present properly this part of the subject to the Imperial authorities, the three Provinces will unite at an early day in a joint representation, on the immense political and commercial importance of the western extension of the projected work.

J. S. McDonald,
L. V. Sicotte,
J. Morris,
W. P. Howland,
Wm. McDougall,
M. J. Tessier,
Thos. D'Arcy McGee,
F. Evantural,
Adam Wilson,
} Representing Canada.

Joseph Howe,
J. McCully,
William Annand,
} Representing Nova Scotia.

S. L. Tilley,
W. H. Steves,
P. Mitchell,
} Representing New Brunswick.

Quebec, 12th September, 1862.

(COPY.)

NO. 2. —MEMORANDUM.

Agreed, at the Conference of the Delegates of Nova Scotia and New Brunswick and the Government of Canada:

I. If it should be concluded that the work shall be constructed and managed by a joint commission of the three Provinces, it shall be constituted in the proportion of two appointed by the Government of Canada, and one each by the Governments of Nova Scotia and New Brunswick; the four to select a fifth before entering upon the discharge of their duties.

II. That a joint delegation proceed with as little delay as possible to England, to arrange with the Imperial Government the terms of the loans, the nature of the security required, the amount to be paid for the transport of troops and mails, and, if possible, to obtain a modification of the terms proposed, to the extent of the interest accruing during the construction of the work.

III. That no surveys be authorized until the laws contemplated shall have been passed, and the joint commissioners appointed. That any profit, or loss, after paying working expenses, shall be divided in proportion to the contribution of the several Provinces.

IV. That such portions of the Railways, now owned by the Governments of Nova Scotia and New Brunswick, which may be required to form part of the Intercolonial Road, shall be worked under such joint authority as may be appointed by the three Provinces. That the rates collected shall be uniform over each respective portion of the Road. That all nett gain or loss, resulting from the working and keeping in repair of any portion of the road constructed by Nova Scotia and New Brunswick, and to be used as a part of the Intercolonial railway, shall be received and borne by the said Provinces respectively, and the surplus, if any, after the payment of interest, shall go in abatement of interest on the whole line between Halifax and the River du Loup.

VI. That Crown Lands, required for the Line, and for Stations, shall be provided by each Province.

(Signed,) THOMAS D'ARCY McGEE,
For Canada.
JOSEPH HOWE,
For Nova Scotia.
S. L. TILLEY.
For New Brunswick.

A Delegation to England, for the adjustment of financial details of great importance, and to secure the sanction of Her Majesty's Government to the arrangements made at Quebec, having been decided upon, it was very desirable that the gentlemen to be selected should be despatched without delay, as the season was advancing, and it was important that the question should, if possible, be ripened for legislation in the Imperial and Colonial Parliaments during this winter. Your Excellency not having returned from Canada, Major-General Doyle was advised to take the next step, of which the following Minute is the official Record:

MINUTE:

At a Council held at the Government House at Halifax, on the 16th day of October, 1862.

Present:

His Honor, Major General Doyle, Administrator of the Government.
The Hon. Mr. Howe, President of the Council.
" Mr. Archibald, Attorney General.
" Mr. McCully, Solicitor General.
" Mr. Anderson, Receiver General.
" Mr. Annand, Financial Secretary.
" Mr. Wier.

The following memoranda [printed on pages 5 and 6] are submitted by the Honourable the President, the Honourable the Solicitor General, and the Honourable the Financial Secretary, and entered on the Minutes as their Report from the conference at Quebec.

Whereupon his Honor the Administrator of the Government, by the advice of the Council, is pleased to appoint the Honourable Joseph Howe as Delegate from Nova Scotia, to represent the interests of the Province in England, in accordance with the resolution adopted on the 12th September by the Intercolonial Conference at Quebec.

His Honor the Administrator, addressed, at the same time, a Despatch to His Grace the Colonial Secretary, which, as it conveys the opinion of an officer of high rank and large experience, as to the importance of the Inter-colonial Road, in a military point of view, we include in this Report:

(Copy.)

No. 92.—Miscella.

Government House, Halifax, N. S.,
16th October, 1862.

My Lord Duke,—

Your Grace has already, I am informed, been made aware by His Excellency the Governor-General of Canada of the result of the delibera-tions which took place at Quebec last month, when the Lieutenant-Governors of Nova Scotia and New Brunswick, with certain Delegates selected from the leading men of these Provinces, assembled there, for the purpose of discussing the subject of the proposed Intercolonial Railroad. I conceive it nevertheless to be my duty to transmit to Your Grace a copy of the Resolu-tions adopted on that occasion, and to inform you that, as it has been deter-mined by the Sister Provinces to send certain members of their Governments to England, for the purpose of arranging with Her Majesty's Ministers the nature of the securities to be given to the Imperial Government, with a view to uniformity of legislation in all the Provinces, I have commissioned the Honorable Joseph Howe to proceed to England, and to put himself in communication with Your Grace, for this purpose.

So much has already been written and said upon the subject of the very great importance of this line of Railroad, and being fully aware of the favorable opinion entertained by Your Grace with reference to it, I feel I should only intrude upon your time if I was to enter generally upon the whole question; but I trust I may be excused in bringing to your notice the very essential benefit, in a military point of view, which would be derived from its construction.

I would take leave to bring to Your Grace's recollection the very great difficulty and enormous expense which was incurred in December last, when I was called upon to pass a force, consisting of upwards of ten thousand men, through the Province of New Brunswick, along the frontier of the State of Maine, into Canada, which, owing to a combination of favorable circumstances, was successfully performed, but which, in time of war, could scarcely be accomplished at all, and certainly not without great loss of life.

Although, in the event of any rupture between Great Britain and the United States, the Metis Road is being prepared for the purpose of enabling troops to proceed to Canada during the winter, out of the reach of any hostile force, it must be borne in mind that the risk of passing large bodies of men over it, during an inclement season, would, as in the former case, be considerable, the delay unavoidably great, and the expense enormous; whereas if railway communications were once established, both troops and munitions of war could at all times be rapidly and safely transported to Canada, and mutual military operations would thereby be vastly facilitated.

Under all these circumstances, the great advantages which would be derived from a Railway such as is in contemplation (provided the site be judiciously selected), cannot, in my opinion, be overestimated.

I have, &c. &c.

(Signed,) HASTINGS DOYLE,
Administrator.

Mr. Howe being about to leave for England, the further progress of the negociation will be described by that gentleman in a subsequent Report.

We have the honor to be,
Your Excellency's
Most obedient,
Very humble servants,
JOSEPH HOWE,
JONATHAN McCULLY.

HALIFAX, N. S. 16th Oct. 1863.

MR. HOWE'S REPORT.

Halifax, February 10, 1863.

MY LORD,

Having, in conformity with the resolution adopted by the Delegates from Nova Scotia and New Brunswick, and the members of the Canadian Government, assembled at Quebec in September, been instructed by His Honor the Administrator to proceed to England to discharge the duties of the mission contemplated by that resolution, it becomes my duty to report:—

That, having communicated with the leader of the Government of New Brunswick, and ascertained that it was his intention to leave by the boat of the 17th October, I took my passage in the Europa, and we went on together, reaching London about the end of the month.

The Delegates from Canada, who it was assumed would come over direct from the St. Lawrence, were not expected for a week after; and we thought it only respectful to wait their arrival, before communicating with the public departments. The next mail from Canada brought me a note from the Honorable Mr. Sicotte, dated at Quebec 24th October, informing me that the Delegates had taken their passages, but had been unexpectedly delayed by some difficulty arising out of the militia question, on the morning of their expected departure, but that they would come on in the next boat, and hoped to join us during the following week.

Under these circumstances, I thought it proper to write to the Duke of Newcastle on the 8th November, informing His Grace that Mr. Tilley and myself were in London—that the Canadian Delegates had been unexpectedly delayed, and leaving it for His Grace to determine whether or not we should wait upon him before their arrival.

We were honored by an interview on the 13th November, and discussed, informally, the resolutions adopted by the Conference at Quebec, and the objects of our mission generally. His Grace appeared, as he had done in 1861, to enter heartily into the views and policy of the Colonial Governments in respect to the Intercolonial Road thought the questions, to be adjusted, were of so much delicacy and importance, that a Delegation could not have been avoided, if there was to be legislation this winter; and pledged to us his cordial co-operation and aid, a pledge which was amply redeemed.

On the 17th November, the Honorable L. V. Sicotte, Attorney General of Canada East, and the Honorable W. P. Howland, Finance Minister, arrived. They paid their respects to the Colonial Secretary on the following day, and the Delegates, after mutual consultation, then commenced the business of their mission in due form.

Though the Colonial Secretary was suffering from severe illness, the Delegates were honored with several interviews, and explained to His Grace the reasons upon which all the resolutions adopted at Quebec were founded, and discussed with him all the questions which came within the purview of his own department; and I am happy to be able to report, that we ultimately obtained His Grace's cheerful acquiescence in all that had been done, and his suggestions as to the best mode of adjusting those questions which naturally came under the control of the Lords Commissioners of the Treasury.

As His Grace's presence in town was no longer necessary, it was arranged that Mr. Howland and Mr. Tilley, the Finance Ministers of their respective Provinces, should discuss those questions with Mr. Hamilton and Mr. Anderson of the Treasury; and that Sir Frederic Rogers, Under Secretary of

State for the Colonies, should form the medium of communication between the Secretary of State and the Delegates, if it became necessary to invoke his Grace's further interference.

Messrs. Howland and Tilley had several interviews with the gentlemen at the Treasury; and, subsequently, all the Delegates met Messrs. Hamilton and Anderson, and discussed with them at large the important questions involved in the guarantee. It was arranged, to our entire satisfaction, that the money should be borrowed by the British Government, and paid over to the Provinces, without any charge for brokerage or commission, other than the ordinary expenses which the British Government are required to pay. This was a very important concession, calculated to save a very large amount of commissions, which would have been lost, had we been left to borrow the money and manage the loan ourselves. Whether the debentures were to bear an interest of 3½ or 4 per cent was left an open question; but it was understood that whatever the rate, the Colonies were to get the benefit of all the money realized, either in the form of principal or premium. On this point we had nothing more to ask.

On another, of equal importance, we were met in a spirit so liberal, as to leave us nothing to desire. The Treasury proposed to give us forty years to repay the loan, by instalments to fall due at decennial periods; and the sums to be repaid at the end of the first two decades were so moderate (£250,000 at the end of ten, and £500,000 at the end of twenty years), as to bring them quite within the compass of the accumulating revenues of all the Provinces.

Upon one point only did there seem to be any difficulty, the question of a sinking fund; and that appeared of sufficient importance to warrant us in seeking an interview with the Right Honorable the Chancellor of the Exchequer. Mr. Gladstone answered our application promptly, received us graciously, and discussed with us the whole subject in a spirit at once frank and conciliatory.

The Chancellor admitted the national character of the work, and the strong claims of the Colonies; but informed us that a guaranteed loan, uncovered by a sinking fund, was a novelty in British legislation;—that it was opposed to the principles he had always advocated, and to the invariable practice of the House of Commons. That the whole stream of precedents was against us, except in the single case of the Turkish loan, which was in the nature of a war subsidy, granted to enable the Sultan to place his army in the field at the outbreak of the Crimean war, and very amply secured. He assured us, that, even if the Cabinet could be got to consent to take down to Parliament a measure without the accustomed provision, they would be outvoted and the measure lost. Under those circumstances, although we exhausted all the arguments which naturally occur to the Colonial mind, they failed to shake the Chancellor's strong conviction, and it was evident that we must accept the guarantee, upon the only terms on which it could be given, or abandon all hopes of being able to accomplish the work.

Assuming, therefore, that provision for a sinking fund must accompany the guarantee, it appeared to be sound policy to endeavor to get the stipulation so modified as to render it but lightly burthensome. It was apparent to us all, that if, in addition to the interest to be paid, the Provinces were expected to accumulate, from the commencement of the work, a sinking fund, to be invested in three per cent consols, while money was worth, at least, six per cent in North America, that a large amount of interest would be lost, and that the burthen would be greater at the outset, and before the road was opened, than the Provinces could bear. In this view of the case all the delegates concurred, and, had not the proposition been modified, we should all, perhaps, have abandoned the negociation.

We stated to the Chancellor, that there was a mode by which the requirements of Parliament would be met, and yet by which the Provinces might be enabled to assume the burthen. It would take four years to build the road, and, at least six more to people the wilderness, through which a large portion of it was to pass. It was unreasonable, therefore, to expect us to begin to repay the money until the object for which it had been borrowed was accomplished. But, if ten years were allowed to elapse before any sinking fund attached, within that period the road would be built, the wilderness peopled, and the population of all the Provinces would be largely increased. They would be enlivened by the animating influences of the work itself, and would, in 1874, be in a condition to bear up buoyantly under obligations, which, in 1864, it might be perilous to assume.

We also pointed out the positive loss which must be entailed upon the Provinces, should they be compelled to invest an accruing sinking fund in the three per cents; and suggested that, as it accumulated, after the end of the first ten years, we should be permitted to invest it in bonds of any of the Colonies, bearing six per cent, or in any other securities, to be approved by Her Majesty's Government.

Upon neither of these points was Mr. Gladstone prepared to give us an answer. He said they were new to him, and he would reflect upon them, with every desire to meet our wishes, if he could; but, being new and very important, he must not be asked to decide without consideration.

On leaving the Chancellor's residence, I felt that the whole matter turned upon the concession of these two points. If they were conceded, the sinking fund was shorn of its terrors, and I was prepared to accept the proposition. If they were not yielded, then I was prepared, so far as Nova Scotia was concerned, to have closed the negociation. Mr. Tilley took precisely the same view of our position. We hoped that we could carry both. The Canadian delegates were less sanguine. They believed that, after long delay, the decision would be against us on both, and that the whole negociation would be ultimately unsuccessful. In this belief they left London for a short visit to Paris, Mr. Tilley and I being free to obtain these concessions, if we could.

We at once put ourselves again in direct communication with His Grace the Duke of Newcastle, and made it clear to His Grace, that, in our judgments, the whole negociation hung upon these two points. Our views were communicated to the Chancellor of the Exchequer, and, on the following day, we had the satisfaction to learn from His Grace that both points had been yielded by Mr. Gladstone.

As the negociations were now virtually brought to a close, and Mr. Tilley was anxious to return home by the steamer from Liverpool on Saturday, 14th December, we arranged with Sir Frederic Rogers that the propositions, as they were now mutually understood, should be sent to us in form —that Mr. Tilley would then accept the guarantee in an official letter, leaving me to do the same, if, on the return of the Canadian Delegates from Paris, they were still dissatisfied, and indisposed to join in such a letter as, in my judgment, was required to meet the case.

The following Treasury Minute was sent to us by Sir Frederic Rogers on the 13th December:

(Copy.)

It is proposed—

1. That Bills shall be immediately submitted to the Legislatures of Canada, Nova Scotia and New Brunswick, authorizing the respective Governments to borrow £3,000,000 under the guarantee of the British Government, in the following proportions: Five-twelfths, Canada; three and a half-twelfths, Nova Scotia; three and a half-twelfths, New Brunswick.

2. But no such loan to be contracted on behalf of any one Colony until corresponding powers have been given to the Governments of the other two Colonies concerned, nor unless the Imperial Government shall guarantee payment of interest on such loan until repaid.

3. The money to be applied to the completion of a railway connecting Halifax with Quebec, on a line to be approved by the Imperial Government.

4. The interest to be a first charge on the consolidated revenue funds of the different Provinces, after the Civil List and the interest of existing debts; and, as regards Canada, after the rest of the six charges enumerated in the 5th and 6th Victoria, Cap. 118, and 3rd and 4th Victoria, Cap. 35 (Act of Union).

5. The debentures to be in series as follow, viz.: £250,000 to be payable ten years after contracting loan; £500,000, twenty years; £1,000,000, thirty years; £1,250,000, forty years. In the event of the debentures, or any of them, not being redeemed by the Colonies at the period when they fall due, the amount unpaid shall become a charge on their respective revenues, next after the loan, until paid. The principal to be repaid as follows:

1*st Decade*, (*say* 1863 *to* 1872 *inclusive*)—£250,000 in redemption of the first series, at or before the close of the first decade from the contracting of the loan.

2*nd Decade*, (*say* 1873 *to* 1882 *inclusive*)—A sinking fund of £40,000, to be remitted annually, being an amount adequate, if invested at 5 per cent compound interest, to provide £500,000 at the end of the decade, the sum to be remitted annually to be invested in the names of trustees in Colonial securities of any of the three Provinces prior to or forming part of, the loan now to be raised, or in such other Colonial securities as Her Majesty's Government shall direct, and the then Colonial Governments shall approve.

3*rd Decade*, (*say* 1883 *to* 1892 *inclusive*)—A sinking fund of £80,000, to be remitted annually, being an amount adequate, if invested at 5 per cent compound interest, to provide £1,000,000 at the end of the decade, the amount, when remitted, to be invested as in the case of the sinking fund for the preceding decade. This amount, when remitted, to be invested as in the preceding decade.

4*th Decade*, (*say* 1893 *to* 1902 *inclusive*)—A sinking fund of £100,000, to be remitted annually, being an amount adequate, if invested at 5 per cent compound interest, to provide £1,250,000, being the balance of the loan at the end of the decade.

Should the sinking fund of any decade produce a surplus, it will go to the credit of the next decade, and, in the last decade, the sinking fund will be remitted or reduced accordingly.

It is, of course, understood that the assent of the Treasury to these arrangements pre-supposes adequate proof of the sufficiency of the Colonial revenues to meet the charges intended to be imposed upon them.

6. The construction of the Railway to be conducted by five commissioners, two to be appointed by Canada, one by Nova Scotia, and one by New Brunswick. These four to choose the remaining commissioner.

7. The preliminary surveys to be effected at the expense of the Colonies, by three engineers, and other officers nominated, two by the commissioners, and one by the Home Government.

8. Fitting provision to be made for the carriage of troops, &c.

Parliament not to be asked for this guarantee until the line and surveys shall have been submitted to, and approved of by, Her Majesty's Government, and until it shall have been shown to the satisfaction of Her Majesty's Government that the line can be constructed without further application for an Imperial guarantee.

(COPY.)

Canada, New Brunswick, and Nova Scotia Inter-colonial Railway Loan.

	1st Decade.	2nd Decade.	3rd Decade.	4th Decade.
CANADA.				
To pay annually for Interest	50,000	45,833⅓	37,500	20,833⅓
At the end of the first ten years a principal sum of	104,583⅓	....	....	....
And after the first ten years a sinking fund per annum	....	16,666⅔	33,333⅓	41,666⅔
Per annum	50,000	62,500	70,833⅓	62,500
And at the end of first ten years a principal sum of	104,583⅓	....	....	....
NEW BRUNSWICK.				
To pay annually for interest	35,000	32,083⅓	26,250	14,583⅓
At the end of the first ten years a principal sum of	72,708⅓	....	....	....
And after the first ten years a sinking fund per annum	....	11,666⅔	23,333⅓	29,166⅔
Per annum	35,000	43,750	49,583⅓	43,750
And at the end of the first ten years a principal sum of	72708⅓	....	....	....
NOVA SCOTIA.				
To pay annually for interest	35,000	32,083⅓	26,250	14,583⅓
At the end of the first ten years a principal sum of	72,708⅓	....	....	....
After the first ten years a sinking fund per annum	....	11,666⅔	23,333⅓	29,166⅔
Per annum	35,000	43,750	49,583⅓	43,750
And at the end of the first ten years a principal sum of	72,708⅓	....	....	....

On receipt of this paper Mr Tilley addressed the following letter to Sir Frederic Rogers :

London, 13th December, 1862.

DEAR SIR,—

As I must return home by this night's mail, Mr. Howe and I have anxiously conferred upon the subject of the Treasury Minute read to us this morning. It accurately describes the terms proposed to the delegates in the various interviews with which we have been honored by His Grace the Colonial Secretary and the Right Honorable the Chancellor of the Exchequer.

As I understand the matter, the delegates have obtained the assent of Her Majesty's Government to every proposition they have submitted, and there is no difference of opinion except as to the single point of the Sinking Fund.

As the Intercolonial Railroad is a work in which the Imperial and Colonial Governments are assumed to have a joint interest—as, in the Provinces, we regard it as indispensible to national defence, and to the transportation to this country, in winter, of breadstuffs in case war with the United States should ever arise, I hope that Mr. Gladstone may be induced to reconsider the matter of the Sinking Fund, and that the Cabinet may be enabled to convince Parliament that, under all the circumstances of this peculiar case, a Sinking Fund should not be insisted upon. But if it is—Mr. Gladstone having consented that the Sinking Fund may be invested in our own or other colonial securities—I will not assume the responsibility of perilling or delaying this great enterprise, by rejecting what the Chancellor of the Exchequer and the Cabinet may regard as an indispensible condition.

I have the honor to be, dear Sir,

Yours truly,

(Signed) S. L. TILLEY.

Sir FREDERIC ROGERS.

Mr. Tilley left London on the 13th December. Messrs. Sicotte and Howland returned early in the following week. To my infinite regret, though nearly all that we had asked had been conceded, and though the single point which had not been yielded was the one which we had been assured Parliament could not yield, and a persistent demand for which must be fatal to the negociation, still the Canadian Delegates appeared to be indisposed to agree to anything which should bind them or the Government they represented to accept the only terms which Her Majesty's Government assured us they could obtain. Having satisfied myself that the views of each delegation must be expressed in a separate paper, I read the following letter to Messrs. Sicotte and Howland, as the expression of my own, and sent it to Sir Frederic Rogers on the 19th December:

(COPY.)

No. 10, Sackville Street, 19th December, 1862.

DEAR SIR,

Messrs. Sicotte and Howland returned from Paris yesterday. I showed them the Treasury Minute, and discussed with them the whole subject which it covers. They will address to you, or to His Grace the Duke of Newcastle, their views, in a separate paper. Nothing remains for me, therefore, but, on the part of the Government of Nova Scotia, to accept the terms proposed, as the best that, under all the circumstances, and after full discussion, can be had.

I concur fully in all that Mr. Tilley has said, or that Messrs. Sicotte and Howland may say, on the subject of the sinking fund. It will give trouble, and must lose us some interest, however skilfully managed. I still hope that Parliament may be induced to rely upon the honor and the ample revenues of the Provinces, for the prompt payment of the instalments, as they become due; but, if that cannot be done, Her Majesty's Government having conceded every other point that we urged, I shall be quite prepared to submit the measure to my colleagues, with my strong recommendation that it be sanctioned by legislation, at the approaching session.

In closing this negociation, which has run over two years, I am quite sure that I express the feelings of all the gentlemen who have been associated with me, when I ask you to convey to His Grace the Duke of Newcastle, our acknowledgements of the urbanity, patience, and readiness of access, by which we have been enabled to discuss this great subject, in all its bearings, with the utmost freedom. To His Grace's hearty co-operation, and personal influence with the Cabinet, the Provinces will largely owe the success of the elevated Colonial policy which it has been the object of our missions to urge.

Believe me,
My dear Sir,
Very truly yours,
(Signed) JOSEPH HOWE.

SIR FREDERIC ROGERS.

This letter was thus acknowledged:

Downing Street, 31st December, 1862.

SIR,—

I am directed by the Duke of Newcastle to acknowledge the receipt of your letter of the 19th of this month, and to acquaint you that it is gratifying to His Grace to learn that the negotiations which have taken place on the subject of the Intercolonial Railway, have been conducted in a manner satisfactory to the delegates sent to England by the Governments of the North American Provinces.

I am, Sir,
Your obedient servant,
FREDERIC ROGERS.

THE HONBLE. JOSEPH HOWE.

The final answer of the Canadian Delegation was not sent in until after I left London. A copy of it has been asked for by telegraph, and promised. In a few days I presume that it will be forwarded, with some official intimation as to the nature of the policy to be pursued by the Government of Canada.

I have the honor to be,
My Lord,
Your Excellency's most obedient,
Very humble servant,
JOSEPH HOWE.

His Excellency,
The Right Honorable,
THE EARL OF MULGRAVE.
&c. &c. &c. &c.

MESSRS. SICOTTE AND HOWLAND'S LETTER.

To His Grace The Duke of Newcastle:

I.

The undersigned, representing the Government of Canada, as delegates specially deputed to arrange with the Imperial Government the terms of the loan to be effected upon the Imperial guarantee offered, as well as the nature of the security, concerning the construction of the International Railway between Halifax and Quebec, have the honor to submit to Your Grace the following memorial:

On the part of the Government of Canada, they must again assert what has been admitted at every period of the negotiations, both by British statesmen and Colonial Governments, that the construction of a Railway connecting the British North American Colonies ought to be regarded as a matter of Imperial concern, and, to use the words of the late Colonial Minister, "as a great national road."

A brief review of the opinions expressed by public men, and of the views entertained by the different Governments of Great Britain and of the Colonies, since 1839, is perhaps necessary now to explain fully the conditions proposed on the part of the Imperial Government, as well as on the part of the Colonial Governments.

In 1839, Lord Durham, in an answer to the Secretary of State for the Colonies, instructing him to turn his attention to the foundation of a road between Halifax and Quebec, in connection with the determination of the Imperial Government to establish steam communication between the former port and Great Britain, strongly recommended the construction of a Railway between the two cities.

During Sir Robert Peel's administration, in 1843, they caused a survey of a Military Road, but, when nearly completed, it was abandoned by the Imperial Government in favor of a Railway.

In 1846, Mr. Gladstone, then Colonial Secretary, organized a survey for the Railroad, at the joint expense of Canada, New Brunswick and Nova Scotia, and the Imperial Government.

Major Robinson, in his report, expresses himself as follows as to the nature and object of such a Railroad:

"In a political and military point of view, the proposed Railroad must "be regarded as becoming a work of necessity."

"The increasing population and wealth of the United States, and the "diffusion of Railroads over their territory, especially in the direction of "the Canadian frontier, renders it absolutely necessary to counterbalance, "by corresponding means, their otherwise preponderating power."

"It is most essential that the Mother Country should be able to keep up "the communication with the Canadas at all times and all seasons. How-"ever powerful England may be at sea, no navy could save Canada from "a land force."

"Weakness invites aggression, and as the Railroad would be a lever of "power, by which Great Britain could bring her strength to bear in the "contest, it is not improbable that its construction would be the means of "preventing a War at some more distant period."

The expense of one year's War would pay the expense for a Railway two or three times over.

In 1848, Earl Grey in transmitting the report of Major Robinson to Lord Elgin, stated in his despatch.

"I have perused this able document with the interest and attention it so "well merits, and I have to convey to you the assurance of Her Majesty's "Government, that we fully appreciate the importance of the proposed un- "dertaking, and entertain no doubt of the great advantages which would "result not only to the Provinces interested in the work, but to the Empire "at large, from the construction of such a Railway; but great as these "advantages would be, it is impossible not to be sensible that the obstacles "to be overcome in providing for so large an expenditure as would be thus "incurred, would be of a very formidable kind."

"Before, therefore, Her Majesty's Government proceed to consider the "question, as to whether any steps should be taken to carry this plan into "effect, it is necessary that we should be informed how the several Pro- "vinces would be prepared to co-operate in its execution."

Lord Elgin declared in his answer to that despatch: "It is obvious that "as soon as Railway communication is extended throughout the Provinces, "a smaller Military force than is now requisite will suffice for their pro- "tection.

"But looking to the anxiety which Your Lordship has repeatedly ex- "pressed, that a diminution in the expenditure incurred by Great Britain "on this account should be effected at the earliest period, I am prepared to "go a step further in this direction, so confident am I that the mere under- "taking of the work in question will tend to raise the Colonists from the "despondency into which recent changes in the commercial policy of the "Empire has plunged them—to unite Provinces to one another and to "the Mother Country, to inspire them with that consciousness of their own "strength and of the value of the connection with Great Britain, which is "their best security against aggression—that I would not hesitate to recom- "mend that an immediate and considerable reduction should take place in "the force stationed in Canada in the event of the execution of the Quebec "and Halifax Railway being determined on."

In 1851, Lord Stanley, in the House of Lords, reviewing the scheme pro- pounded by Earl Grey, stated in a speech which was accepted by the colo- nies as the expression of the opinions and feelings of the people of England. "He held, therefore, that the establishment of a line of communication "between Halifax and Quebec for a distance of about 700 miles through an "exclusively British territory, rendering two points, and two points essen- "tial for the power of this country, which are now separated by a vast "extent of wilderness on the one side, and by a difficult, and for a great "portion of the year, frozen coast on the other, rendering their communica- "tion from being what they now are, most uncertain, most difficult, and "most dilatory—rendering it rapid, easy and constant—that, he said, was "an object itself of primary importance to the interests, and to the Im- "perial power of this country on the continent of America."

"But it was also a matter of incalculable importance that we should open "to the teeming thousands and millions we were pouring out from this "country, where they were unable to obtain a livelihood, that we should "open to them a home in a healthy climate, and within a very limited dis- "tance from our own shores, which did not exceed a twelve days' passage by "steam, and the rapidity of that passage was every day increasing, it was "of the highest importance whether we looked at it as affording a relief for "our pauperism, or an increase of our power in those regions, that we had "eleven or twelve millions of acres of unoccupied lands, fertile, and pos- "sessed of great mineral wealth, and which at the same time would be the "means of extending our Military power, and securing the permanence of "our empire in America. This was no ordinary case of a Railway project "where the question very properly might be, would the line pay or not? "but it is a Railway which even in a pecuniary sense, he had sanguine ex- "pectations would pay, if they took into consideration not merely the traffic "on the Railway, but the adjuncts they would raise by the formation of it.

" But he said if it would not pay one shilling for the £100 in a pecuniary " point of view for the next ten years to come, the interposition of this " Country, not for the purpose of involving itself in an enormous and need- " less expense, but for the purpose of aiding with its credit, if not by more " than its credit, those who were anxious to the utmost of their power, and " even beyond their power, not for a local but for an Imperial object, this " was a subject well worthy of the consideration of the Imperial Parlia- " ment, and was not to be looked upon as a matter of pounds, shillings and " pence.

" Now, he felt that to grant our aid was a wise, a sound, and even an " economical course in the end, even though, in the first instance, it would " involve an outlay, and sure he was that it would confer immense benefits " on the Colony, and bestow incalculable advantages on this Country itself, " and confirm its territorial power in North America.

" And if the Noble Earl would only say which course he should be pre- " pared to take, and if the Government would give any sanction and assist- " ance for the execution of what these Colonies could not accomplish unas- " sisted, although he believed a comparatively small aid on the part of the " Government, or its liberal guarantee for the capital required, on account " of which guarantee they would never be called upon to pay a single shil- " ling, such an amount of assistance from the Government, he firmly be- " lieved, would enable the great work to be carried to a successful comple- " tion, and equally certain he was that unless our Government and our Par- " liament did interfere, these advantages would be indefinitely postponed, " the communication between two most important points would be perma- " nently cut off, the stream of emigration would continue to be directed as " it was now directed from this country and Ireland, not to our own colo- " nies, but to the territories of the United States; the communication be- " tween Halifax and Quebec would ultimately be through the United States, " be wholly dependent upon them, and liable at any moment to be cut off " in the case of hostilities; while the United States would be able to reap " all the advantages of the transit in times of peace.

" Now we had the option whether we should give to the United States " these great advantages, and, at the same time, deprive the subjects of this " country of the opportunity of receiving a useful and most valuable popu- " lation settling in our colonies, and by their emigration relieving the over- " burdened Mother Country of its surplus labor; or whether we would, by " a prompt and liberal course of action, which would ultimately cost us " nothing, enable our dependencies to complete that which would cement a " stronger union between our North American possessions, and to teach " them to feel that they were regarded by the Imperial Government and " Parliament as an integral portion of the Empire. On the other hand, we " beg to recall to your Grace's recollection the facts that—

The Legislature of the Colonies and their Governments have always represented the Road as a necessary means for the defence of the country and as a work of national concern.

On the 6th January, 1849, the Legislative Council of New Brunswick passed a series of resolutions, from which the following extracts are made:

" Viewing the relative positions of the North American Colonies, and the " great importance, in a national point of view, of improving the facilities " for mutual intercourse, we consider it a matter of the greatest moment for " the permanency of British interests on this continent, that a Railway " should be laid down to connect the lower Provinces with the interior of " Canada.

" We believe that no other measure can be devised which will so certainly " consolidate the Colonies, and perpetuate our connection with Great Bri- " tain; while without it we fear that our position, as Colonies, will be of " short duration.

"We think the plain broad question on this subject is: Do the people of "England wish to retain the North American Colonies, or not? If they "do, the Trunk Railway is indispensible, and should be completed at any "cost."

On the 1st May, 1858, the Legislature of Nova Scotia addressed Her Majesty as follows:

"This great enterprise, of national no less than colonial importance, has "been, through many years, pressed upon the consideration of your Ma-"jesty's Government.

"The benefits of the measure, both in its national and colonial relations, "are acknowledged.

"The gigantic work has been facilitated by the efforts and expenditure of "the provinces, but its accomplishment is beyond their unaided resources, "and on the efficient assistance of your Majesty's Government depends the "great result."

In 1858, the Legislature of Canada passed the following resolutions:

"1. That the construction of an Intercolonial Railway, connecting the "provinces of New Brunswick and Nova Scotia with Canada, has long been "regarded as a matter of national concern, and ought earnestly to be "pressed on the consideration of the Imperial Government.

"2. That during several months of the year, intercourse between the "United Kingdom and Canada can only be carried on through the territory "of the United States of America, and that such dependence on and exclu-"sive relations with a foreign country cannot, even in time of peace, but "exercise an important and unwholesome influence on the state of Canada "as a portion of the Empire, and may tend to establish elsewhere that "identity of interest which ought to exist between the Mother Country and "her colonies.

"That while the house implicitly relies on the repeated assurance of the "Imperial Government, that the strength of the Empire would be put "forth to secure this Province against external aggression, it is convinced "that such strength cannot be sufficiently exerted during a large portion of "the year, from the absence of sufficient means of communication, and that "should the amicable relations which at present so happily exist between "Great Britain and the United States be ever disturbed, the difficulty of "access to the ocean during the winter months might seriously endanger "the safety of the Province.

"4. That in view of the speedy opening up of the Territories, now occu-"pied by the Hudson Bay Company, and of the development and settle-"ment of the vast regions between Canada and the Pacific Ocean, it is es-"sential to the interests of the Empire at large, that a highway extending "from the Atlantic Ocean westward should exist, which should at once "place the whole British possessions in America within the ready access "and easy protection of Great Britain, whilst, by the facilities for internal "communication thus afforded, the prosperity of those great dependencies "would be promoted, their strength consolidated, and added to the strength "of the Empire, and their permanent union with the Mother Country "secured.

In 1861, the Colonies pressed again upon the Imperial Government the advantages and necessity of constructing the Railway.

Their Delegates strongly urged that—

"Without that Road the Provinces are dislocated, and almost incapable "of defence for a great portion of the year, except at such a sacrifice of life "and property, and at such an enormous cost to the Mother Country, as "makes the small contribution which she is asked to give towards its con-

" struction, sink into insignificance. With that Railroad we can concentrate " our forces on the menaced parts of our frontier; guard the citadels and " works which have been erected by Great Britain at vast expense, cover " our cities from surprise, and hold our own till reinforcements can be sent " across the sea, while without the Railway, if an attack were made in win- " ter, the Mother Country could put no Army worthy of the National honor, " and adequate to the exigency on the Canadian frontier, without a positive " waste of treasure far greater than the principal of the sum, the interest of " which she is asked to contribute or rather to risk.

" The British Government have built expensive citadels at Halifax, Que- " bec and Kingston, and have stores of munitions and warlike materials in " them, but their feeble garrisons will be inadequate for their defence, unless " the provincial forces can be concentrated in and around them. An enter- " prising enemy would carry them by *coups de main* before they could be " reinforced from England, and once taken, the ports and roadsteads which " they have been erected to defend, would not be over safe for the naval " armaments sent out too late for their relief.

" That the subject should be looked upon and dealt with mainly to the " consideration of permanent connection between Great Britain and the " Provinces, and the relative positions of England and the United States " in the event of hostilities between them."

The Imperial Government gave a final answer to all these demands and considerations, by the Despatch of Your Grace of the 12th April, 1862, in which Your Grace says:

" I much regret to inform you that, after giving the subject the best con- " sideration, Her Majesty's Government have not felt themselves at liberty " to concur in this mode of assistance. Anxious, however, to promote, as " far as they can, the important object of completing the great line of Rail- " way communication on British ground, between the Atlantic and the " westernmost parts of Canada, and to assist the Provinces in a scheme " which would so materially promote their interests, Her Majesty's Gov- " ernment are willing to offer to the Provincial Governments an imperial " guarantee of interest, towards enabling them to raise, by public loan, if " they should desire it, at a moderate rate, the requisite funds for construct- " ing the Railway."

The Colonies held in consequence a conference at Quebec, in September, and then by their delegates agreed:

" 1. That whilst they have learned with very great regret that Her Ma- " jesty's Imperial Government has finally declined to sanction the proposals " made on behalf of these Provinces in December, 1861, and at previous " periods, they at the same time acknowledge the consideration exhibited " in substituting the proposal of 'An Imperial Guarantee of Interest tow- " 'ards enabling them to raise by Public Loan, if they should desire it, at " 'a moderate rate, the requisite funds for constructing the Railway.' "

" 2. That with an anxious desire to bind the Provinces more closely to- " gether, to strengthen their connection with the Mother Country, to pro- " mote their common commercial interests, and to provide facilities essential " to the public defences of these Provinces as integral parts of the Empire, " the undersigned are prepared to assume under the Imperial Guarantee " the liability for the expenditure necessary to construct this great work."

" 3. That in arriving at this conclusion the undersigned have been greatly " influenced by the conviction that the construction of the Road between " Halifax and Quebec, must supply an essential link in the chain of an " unbroken highway extending through British territory from the Atlantic " to the Pacific, in the completion of which every Imperial interest in North " America is most deeply involved."

II.

The Colonies have declared their willingness to assume the whole liability of the cost of the Road, provided they are assisted in raising the requisite funds for its construction at a moderate rate of interest by the Imperial Guarantee. It may fairly be said that the proposal now is not of a Loan of Imperial moneys to the Colonies for Colonial purposes only, but of a mode, involving no actual liability to the Imperial Government, to facilitate the construction of a great National work in the interest of the Empire as well as of the Colonies.

The only question involved as regards Great Britain is the sufficiency of the security offered by the Colonies to cover this distant liability resulting from the Imperial Guarantee.

If their past condition, compared with the present, does not establish fully their ability to repay the Loan in the periods proposed, such a comparison would only prove, more strongly than any other fact, that this admittedly necessary work of military defence ought to be executed by the Imperial Government alone. But to make evident the ampleness of the security offered by the Colony, it is sufficient to compare the Revenue of the Colony in 1842, when the first Imperial Guaranteed Loan was effected, with the Revenues in 1861.

In 1842, it was £ sterling, in 1861, it is £ sterling, after deduction of the cost of collection.

After several interviews with your Grace, and the Chancellor of the Exchequer, when the conditions of the Loan, the nature of the security, and the arrangements of a Sinking Fund were discussed without coming to any positive understanding, the Delegates have now been officially informed that the Imperial Guarantee will be given on certain conditions stated in the annexed Document.

The Delegates regret to state that, in their opinion, some of these conditions are of a nature to render the Imperial Guarantee of no advantage, and other to render its availableness so remote, or encumbered with such difficulties, that the Colonies could not accept it, as an assistance towards an undertaking, and a measure to provide facilities essential to the future defence of the Provinces as integral parts of the Empire.

The stipulation that the Loan is to be the first charge after the interest of existing debts, seems to them shaped so as to operate against the payment of other debts coming due before the repayment of the Loan.

The annual repayment of the Loan renders the period of payment much shorter than the period proposed, and besides the loss it involves, it deprives the Colony of a large sum which, employed during such a period towards internal improvements, would afford a greater security than this annual payment by the development of the resources and of the wealth of the Country. In any arrangement, the Colonies ought not to be fettered by conditions of payment through any form of Sinking Fund, which would make this Imperial Guarantee an impediment to future internal improvement, while, by increasing the rate of interest and by the expenses and loss incurred in its management, the Imperial Guarantee would thus cease to be of any real aid and advantage.

The investment of these annual payments into Colonial Securities will not give a better security than the engagement of the Colonial Government to pay a fixed sum at a fixed period.

These investments into Colonial Securities, as Her Majesty's Government shall direct and the Colonial Governments shall approve, will lead to difficulties which, if not of a graver character than those that have already arisen out of the disposal of the Sinking Fund, created for the first Imperial Guarantee, fully satisfy the Delegates that these arrangements are not more favorable than the former.

The experience of Canada is strongly adverse to a Sinking Fund. It created annoyances and difficulties, made the rate of interest higher than she would have paid by borrowing on her unassisted credit.

The Delegates are informed that it is of course understood that the assent of the Treasury to these arrangements presupposes adequate proof of the sufficiency of the Colonial resources to meet the charges intended to be imposed upon them.

When after more than 20 years negotiations the offer of an Imperial Guarantee was made, the Colonies had some right to believe that the sufficiency of their Revenues to meet these increased charges was known and acknowledged, as all information which they could give are already in the possession of the Treasury, and which are set forth in the fullest detail in the statistical table annually published by Her Majesty's Government. No Survey, no Legislation can take place before the Colonies are made aware that adequate proof has been made of the sufficiency of their revenues to meet the intended charges, and it would be important for the Colonies to be informed, at the earliest period, what further proof is wanted.

The 8th condition is, that fitting provision is to be made for the carriage of troops, &c. &c.

If it is meant that the troops are to be carried free of any charge, the Delegates must observe that when this was offered by the Colonies, it was as a part of the scheme then proposed, that England should contribute half the costs of the construction of the Road.

When it is now proposed that the whole cost should be borne by the Colonies, it cannot be expected that they must also relieve the Imperial Government from all expenditure attending the transport of troops, &c.

All these conditions presuppose that the Imperial Government has no interest to serve or no policy to uphold in the construction of this great Railway, that the Colonies must be treated as any other Government asking a Loan from the Imperial Treasury. Proof is required as it is enacted from any unknown debtor, as to the sufficiency of his means to meet his engagement. With an ordinary debtor, when this sufficiency is established he may do what he pleases with the moneys borrowed. But in this instance the funds are to be applied to an undertaking admitted by all to afford an immense developement to the wealth of the Creditor, enabling him to maintain more efficiently his power and supremacy, with the control even of directing the location of this work where in his opinion it will secure all these advantages most efficiently, although the costs to the Debtor may be much increased and the pecuniary advantages made much less, if not a great loss thereby.

The Treasury proposes another condition which must greatly delay all the arrangements, and may, after all the expenses attending the requisite Surveys, the trouble and the difficulties of carrying the necessary Legislation in the different Colonial Legislatures, render all this trouble, all this expenditure, all this Legislation, useless and of no avail, leaving certainly a strong feeling of dissatisfaction in the minds of the inhabitants of the Colonies.

The Imperial Government is not to be asked for this guarantee until the line and the surveys shall have been submitted to and approved by Her Majesty's Government, and until it shall have been proved to the satisfaction of Her Majesty's Government that the line can be constructed without further application for an Imperial guarantee.

The proposed guarantee is limited by the Treasury to three millions of pounds. It is possible that the Railroad may cost half a million or more above this fixed sum of three millions, and this by the fact of a selection of route chosen for its military advantages, and upon considerations certainly as Imperial as Colonial. And then the Colonies, before obtaining this guarantee, must prove to parties not always shewing too much confidence in their wealth, that the line can be constructed without further application for an Imperial guarantee.

Another period of many years will probably elapse before the discussions upon this point close.

The Schedule presupposes that the rate of interest is fixed by the Treasury at 4 per cent, while it was demanded by the Delegates after consultation with the fiscal agents of the Province, that the rate should be fixed at 3½ per cent, and that the Debentures should bear that rate of interest.

The surveys and the selection of the route must be settled as preliminary proceedings to any legislation prepared to carry out the offer of the Imperial guarantee in the Colonial Legislature.

By the proposal of the Treasury it is only after the surveys and after the selection of the route that the Provinces can act in regard to this guarantee, if the cost is established at no more than three millions, and when information is given to the Colonies that their resources are judged sufficient to bear the charge.

If the cost of construction is above three millions, proof must be made to the satisfaction of Her Majesty's Government that the line can be constructed without further application for an Imperial guarantee. Pending the discussion which may follow during a long period to establish this fact or this possibility, no action, no legislation can be adopted.

III.

Some of these conditions and demands are a strange commentary upon the official statement made by Earl Grey in 1848. "Her Majesty's Government fully appreciates the importance of the proposed undertaking, and entertain no doubt of the great advantages which would result, not only to the provinces interested in the work, but to the Empire at large, from the construction of such a Railway, but before proceeding to consider the question whether steps should be taken by Her Majesty's Government to carry this plan into effect, it was necessary that they should be informed how the several provinces were disposed to co-operate in its execution."

These demands rather ungracefully unsay the eloquent words of Earl Derby, "That to grant an Imperial aid was a wise, a sound, and even an economical course in the end, even though in the first instance it would involve an outlay, and sure he was that it would confer immense benefits to the Colonies, and bestow incalculable advantages on this Country itself, and confirm its territorial power in North America."

The question of the Public Defences of the Colonies as integral parts of the Empire, the question of the maintenance, of the extension of the political and social influence of England, over the whole of her immense possessions in North America, the economical questions of so vast magnitude to the welfare of the Nation, the question of unemployed capital, of surplus labor, underlie every link of the great and national road, which Canada is anxious to build by the largest and most liberal contribution, from the Atlantic to the Pacific.

She had a just right to ask the co-operation of Great Britain, and when she only demands for an advance of guarantee, which can, by no eventualities, involve the liability of a single half-penny, to use the language of Earl Derby, she has certainly fair grounds to expect a prompt and liberal course of action.

If the different groups of population, spread over British America, and which will numerate at least 12 or 15 millions in twenty-five years, are allowed to proceed in different directions, to have no common tendencies, without any centralization of their political existence, no other bond but their disjointed interests fostered by different commercial policies, and settled upon principles of localities, they must continue weak and powerless, and an easy prey for the powerful republic girdled round these Colonies.

Bind all these small communities by closer intercourse, make a whole, strong by its unity of interests, of tendencies, of political organization, of common views; create by commercial relations mutual interests amongst themselves and with, England, direct the minds towards a general and comprehensive policy you will thus benefit the industry, the wealth of England, extend your power of civilization, and lay the foundation of large and important states friendly and grateful.

The Canadian Government does not press this undertaking, because it is popular with their people. On the contrary, they have to encounter a strong and popular opposition, but fully appreciating the strength and the importance it will eventually give their Country, and more particularly the facilities it will provide for the public defences of their part of the Empire, they have not hesitated to adopt a policy, which appeared to them sound, highly national and conducive to the greatness and the defence of the Empire at large.

As a measure of defence Canada will cheerfully bear her share of the large burden imposed by the construction of the road. But if the policy of the Imperial Government, in relation to this work, is practically a declaration that they are not disposed to treat it as a measure of national concern and of public defence of a portion of the Empire, the enterprise will not become more popular.

The views and the policy involved and following out of the conditions attached to this, so distant liability of the Imperial Exchequer, are so much at variance with the views and the policy entertained by Canada, that the undersigned have considered themselves bound to review these so long pending negotiations, and to contrast the views of the Colonies as to the military and Imperial character of the work, with the Imperial policy refusing to contribute towards it, and arranging not an advance of money, but of a simple guarantee which the work alone would sufficiently protect, in a manner illiberal, obstructive, and which refuses to acknowledge any corresponding duty on the part of the Mother Country.

They will hasten to submit to their Government the conditions and arrangements proposed by the Imperial Government, to carry out the offer of an Imperial guarantee, with the hope that upon the pressing instances of the Colonies, this aid of an Imperial guarantee will be given in the manner explained by the delegates at their different interviews with Your Grace and the Treasury.

These conditions urged by the delegates and detailed in the annexed paper, in enabling the Colonies to borrow the requisite funds at the low rate of 3½ per cent, would render the Imperial guarantee a real and tangible assistance, accepted as an equivalent to the contribution of the Imperial Government towards a work of national concern and a measure of public defence. The actual and future wealth of the colonies are ample and sufficient securities of the Imperial Exchequer against the possibilities even the most remote, of any loss, and a satisfactory proof that the road would be constructed if these conditions were accepted.

London, 23rd December, 1862.

(Signed) L. V. SICOTTE,
W. P. HOWLAND.

It is proposed by the Delegates—

1. That the loan shall be for £3,000,000 sterling;
2. That the liabilities of each colony shall be apportioned as follows:

£1,250,000 for Canada,
£875,000 for New Brunswick,
£875,000 for Nova Scotia.

3. The debentures shall bear interest at the rate of 3½ per cent;
4. The interest shall be paid half yearly in London, on the first of May and on the first of November;

5. That the sum borrowed shall be repaid in four instalments:

£250,000 in 10 years,
£500,000 in 20 years,
£1,000,000 in 30 years,
£1,250,000 in 40 years.

6. The net profits of the road shall be applied towards the extinction of the debt;

7. That the loan shall be the first charge upon the revenue of each colony after the existing debts and charges;

8. That the Imperial Government shall have the right to select one of the engineers to be appointed to make the surveys for the location of the road;

9. That the selection of the line shall rest with the Imperial Government;

10. That if it is concluded that the work is to be constructed and managed by a joint commission, it shall be constituted in the following proportions: Canada shall appoint two of the Commissioners, New Brunswick and Nova Scotia each one;

These four shall name a fifth before entering upon the discharge of their duties;

11. That such portions of the railways now owned by the Governments of New Brunswick and Nova Scotia, which may be required to form part of the Intercolonial Road, will be worked under the above commission;

12. That all net gain or loss resulting from the working and keeping in repair of any portions of the roads constructed by Nova Scotia and New Brunswick, and to be used as a part of the Intercolonial Road, shall be received and borne by these Provinces respectively, and the surplus, if any, after the payment of interest, shall go in abatement of interest of the whole line between Halifax and Riviere-du-Loup.

13. That the rates shall be uniform over each respective portion of the road;

14. That Crown Lands required for the Railway or Stations shall be provided by each Province.

(Copy.)

MR. TILLEY TO SIR F. ROGERS.

Provincial Secretary's Office,
Fredericton, N. B., January 5th, 1863.

Dear Sir,

Just before leaving London I received the copy of the paper you read to me at the Colonial Office on the morning of the 13th December last, as embodying the terms on which the Duke of Newcastle and Mr. Gladstone would be prepared to propose to Parliament an Imperial guarantee of the Railway loan of £3,000,000.

In the letter accompanying the memorandum you state that the 4th clause is not altered so as to meet my objections, as Mr. Hamilton thought it best that I should receive the paper as it stood, and that I could make my observations upon that section.

As worded, the provisions of section 4 if embodied in an act of our Legislature, would change the character of our debentures now outstanding. Such a measure could not be sanctioned by the Government or Legislature, and I am confident it will not be insisted on when understood by Mr. Gladstone. The proposed loan must stand as a first charge on the consolidated revenue after the civil list and existing legal liabilities including *principal* as well as *interest.*

During one of the interviews with which Mr. Howe and I were favored by Mr. Hamilton, it was understood that if the Imperial guarantee was given, the debentures would be issued by the Lords Commissioners of Her Majesty's Treasury, and these Commissianers would act as trustees of this loan and sinking fund. This arrangement is only indirectly referred to in the memorandum transmitted to me on the 13th December. You will please obtain the sanction of the Treasury to an additional section containing this proposal.

It is possible that these matters have all been arranged by the Canadian and Nova Scotta delegrtes before leaving, and the necessary records made. If so an answer to this letter will not be necessary.

I am, &c.

(Signed) S. L. TILLEY.

Sir FREDERIC ROGERS,
Colonial Office.

(COPY.)

Nova Scotia.—No. 4.

Downing Street,
24th January, 1863.

MY LORD,—

I have the honor to transmit to you herewith a copy of a memorandum which Messrs Sicotte and Howland, the Delegates from Canada on the subject of the Inter-colonial Railway have addressed to me on their departure from England.

I have, &c.

(Signed) NEWCASTLE.

The Right Honorable
THE EARL OF MULGRAVE.

(COPY.)

Nova Scotia.—No. 10.

Downing Street,
31st January, 1863.

MY LORD,—

With reference to my despatch No. 4, of the 24th of January, I have the honor to transmit to Your Lordship a copy of a minute by the Secretary to the Treasury upon two questions raised in the annexed letter from Mr. Tilley, the delegate of New Brunswick, on the subject of the proposed loan for the construction of the Intercolonial Railway, viz., the mode in which the loan should be raised, and the extent to which it should form a first charge on the Provincial revenue.

I have, &c.

(Signed) NEWCASTLE.

Lieut. Governor
The Right Honorable
THE EARL OF MULGRAVE, &c. &c. &c.

(Copy.)

With reference to the two questions raised by Mr. Tilley on the stipulations embodied in the memorandum relating to the proposed Loan for the construction of an Inter-colonial Railway, the Treasury considers that an answer should be sent to the following effect:

1. Her Majesty's Government never contemplated acquiring a precedence over existing engagements of the Colonial Governments, whether for interest or principal; but the assent of the Treasury to the arrangement, as stated in Article V, presupposes adequate proof of the sufficiency of the Colonial revenues to meet the charges imposed upon them, which charges would comprise not only the Civil List and the accruing interest of any existing debt standing in priority to the proposed Railway Loan, but also any payment of principal standing in the same priority which may fall due within the period at the expiration of which the Railway Loan is required to be fully liquidated, as well as the current interest and the decennial accumulations for extinction of principal of the proposed Railway Loan.

No statement of revenue or liabilities which would afford this evidence has yet been exhibited to Her Majesty's Government.

2. In the event of the proposed arrangement being carried into effect, the Treasury will not object to issue the debentures upon the precedent of the Canada Guaranteed Loan of 1843, under the hands of the Lords Commissioners, and to authorize one of their officers to act as trustee, together with a nominee of the Colony, for the investment, in their joint names, of the instalments remitted from time to time on account of sinking fund, provided such a course should be deemed advisable by the Colonial Governments.

(Signed) G. A. H. 23rd Jany. 1863.

www.ingramcontent.com/pod-product-compliance
Lightning Source LLC
LaVergne TN
LVHW011138110826
845150LV00008B/2397

* 9 7 8 1 4 1 8 1 9 4 2 4 6 *